SQUADRONS!

No. 22

The Douglas

BOSTON & HAVOC
- The Australians -

Phil H. LISTEMANN

ISBN: 979-1096490-12-7

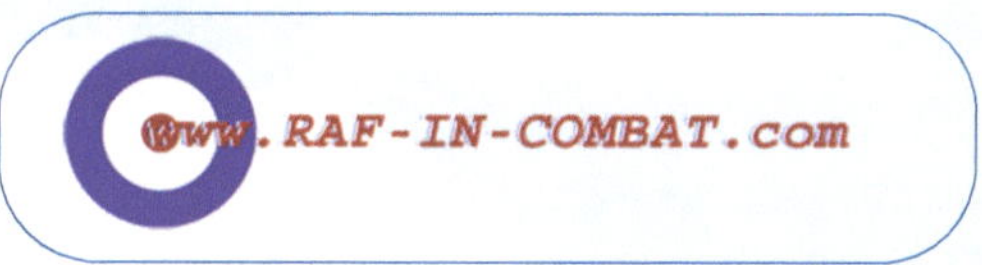

updated January 2018

Colour profiles: Gaetan Marie/Bravo Bravo Aviation

Contributors & Acknowledgments:
Aviation Heritage Museum of Western Australia

GLOSSARY OF TERMS

PERSONEL :
(AUS)/RAF: Australian serving in the RAF
(BEL)/RAF: Belgian serving in the RAF
(CAN)/RAF: Canadian serving in the RAF
(CZ)/RAF: Czechoslovak serving in the RAF
(NFL)/RAF: Newfoundlander serving in the RAF
(NL)/RAF: Dutch serving in the RAF
(NZ)/RAF: New Zealander serving in the RAF
(POL)/RAF: Pole serving in the RAF
(RHO)/RAF: Rhodesian serving in the RAF
(SA)/RAF: South African serving in the RAF
(US)/RAF - RCAF : American serving in the RAF or RCAF

RANKS
G/C : Group Captain
W/C : Wing Commander
S/L : Squadron Leader
F/L : Flight Lieutenant
F/O : Flying Officer
P/O : Pilot Officer
W/O : Warrant Officer
F/Sgt : Flight Sergeant
Sgt : Sergeant
Cpl : Corporal
LAC : Leading Aircraftman

OTHER
ATA: Air Transport Auxiliary
CO : Commander
DFC : Distinguished Flying Cross
DFM : Distinguished Flying Medal
DSO : Distinguished Service Order
Eva. : Evaded
ORB : Operational Record Book
OTU : Operational Training Unit
PoW : Prisoner of War
PAF: Polish Air Force
RAF : Royal Air Force
RAAF : Royal Australian Air Force
RCAF : Royal Canadian Air Force
RNZAF : Royal New Zealand Air Force
SAAF : South African Air Force
s/d: Shot down
Sqn : Squadron
† : Killed

The Boston III and the A-20G

This Douglas design was built in so many versions, covering so many missions, that to simplify things, only the Boston III and A-20G will be introduced here.

The Douglas Boston was born as the Douglas DB-7, the production version of a prototype, the Model 7B. Although the prototype crashed while being tested by the French, the French had seen enough to place an order of 100 aircraft, modified to meet their particular requirements, on 15 February 1939, only eleven days after the crash of the prototype. Another contract for 170 with more powerful engines was signed on 14 October 1939, and a third contract was signed six days later for 100 examples of the improved DB-7A (DB-71 in French terminology) with its revised and larger tail. The USAAC also showed an interest in the aircraft and decided to buy a derivative that became the A-20A Havoc.

The British, looking for a replacement for the Bristol Blenheim, as it had become abundantly clear that that type was severely outclassed, followed suit. The British model (DB-7B) was similar to the French DB-71 and 300 were ordered, as Boston Mk.Is, in two separate contracts, the first 150 on 20 February 1940 and the second on 17 April. As the French received priority, the British did not expect their aircraft to be delivered before 1941. However, in the meantime, France collapsed and they subsequently handed their orders over to the British before the Armistice was signed. Therefore, as only the French DB-7s were under production, the remaining French DB-7s were taken on charge first and took over the denomination of Boston Mk.I. The French DB-71 became the Boston II, thus obliging the British Air Ministry to revise the denomination of the variant ordered by the RAF. These became Boston Mk IIIs. These direct orders received the serials W8252-W8401 (150) and Z2155-Z2304 (150). The RAF would also inherit two contracts of the French equivalent of the DB-7B placed in May 1940. These were intended to receive the DB-73 designation. Douglas and Boeing had received an order of 240 aircraft each. The British eventually allocated serials AL263-AL502 for Boeing-built Bostons and AL668-AL907 for those coming off the Douglas production line. All were built to British specifications and were very similar to the Boston IIIs of the first batches. In the meantime, the USAAC continued to order the A-20, for its own use and Lend-Lease export, with the next version being the A-20B which was very similar to the A-20A. The A-20C soon followed. This was actually a Boston III built to US specifications and was otherwise very similar to the British variant. Those A-20Cs received by the RAF would eventually be known as Boston IIIAs. Finally, the USAAF, in 1943, added the A-20G to its inventory. The A-20G became the most numerous variant constructed. The main difference was the addition a solid gun nose in place of the conventional glazed nose of the earlier versions. Later sub-variants were also fitted with a Martin dorsal turret armed with two 0.50-in calibre machine guns. The British did not acquire this variant for operational service.

The British ordered the Boston as a replacement for the Blenheim light bomber which was approaching obsolescence in 1940. The Boston was a fine alternative and proved rather versatile as the RAF also used it as a night fighter and intruder. The British Bostons was equipped with four 0.303-in calibre machine guns in the nose which were rarely used when the Boston was flown as a conventional light bomber. The Boston III became the mainstay of the RAF day bomber squadrons in the UK with 2 Group Bomber Command in 1941-1942, but was also widely used in North Africa and Italy.

The first Boston IIIs shortly after their delivery to No. 22 Squadron at Richmond, Australia, with the roundels freshly painted to replace the orange triangle of the Dutch. *(AHM & WA)*

BOSTONS FOR THE RAAF

The introduction of the Boston into the RAAF's inventory was a pure accident. While selected by the RAF for its operations in Europe as a popular replacement for the Bristol Blenheim in the light bomber role, the RAAF preferred in the Army support role the Vultee Vengeance dive bomber at the light of the European operations (Wirraways were used temporarily in this role till proper dive bombers could be acquired).

After the signature of the Rome-Berlin-Tokyo Axis treaty in September 1940, and the taking control of French Indochina, the threat of the Japanese Empire and its ambitions over all of Asia was taken seriously by the other major powers in the region: the British Empire, the Americans and the Dutch. All began to reinforce their military presence in the region and much military equipment was purchased to bolster their strength. In 1941 the Dutch signed various contracts for American combat aircraft. Among them was a contract for 48 Douglas DB-7Cs (signed on 10 October 1941). The deliveries were planned to take place between April and May 1942. However, with the Japanese making their move in December 1941, the situation changed and an urgent need for aircraft arose. The Americans diverted many aircraft from British orders for their own use and many Boston IIIs under production for the RAF were seized by the US government in the days following Pearl Harbor. As the military situation rapidly worsened, the Dutch pressed the US to deliver aircraft as quickly as possible. As many Boston IIIs were being seized, the Dutch accepted an American offer to deliver 32 former RAF Boston IIIs as an interim measure. Therefore 32 ex-RAF Boston IIIs were soon crated and shipped to the Netherlands East Indies. The first six arrived on board the Dutch freighter *Kota Baroe* on 28 February 1942, a few days before the Netherlands East Indies surrendered to the Japanese. These fell in to Japanese hands. Of the other 26 aircraft, 22 were en route to South East Asia, and four were still in the US. Those four never left the country. The 22 Bostons in transit were diverted to Australia where they arrived in five batches at Melbourne in March and April 1942. From Melbourne they were shipped in their crates for assembly at nearby Laverton and brought up to RAAF standards as, even though they were initially RAF Boston IIIs, they had all been modified to Dutch standards, which included instruments and wording in Dutch. The Dutch markings would also have to be painted over. These aircraft were allocated the serials **A28-1 to A28-22**.

With a Japanese invasion becoming a real possibility, there was no sense in keeping these bombers in storage. They were to be put into service as soon as possible, preferably with the Dutch who had found refuge in Australia after March 1942. With the formation of No. 18 (NEI) Squadron within the RAAF as a bomber unit, ten of the Bostons were initially allocated to the Dutch alongside a few B-25 Mitchells. Another ten went to No. 22 Squadron RAAF. However, the Dutch soon decided to continue with just the B-25, of which many were in transit to Australia, leaving the entire batch of Bostons for 22 Squadron. They were actually welcomed to replace 22's Ansons and Wirraways with a modern type but only as an interim. The employment of the Boston was indeed intended to be short until such time as the Vengeance became available in sufficient numbers. The invasion never happe-

4

ned and, unexpectedly, the RAAF discovered a new role more suited to the Boston than the defensive tasking it had been given so far. At the end of 1942, the Allies were on the offensive in New Guinea and the Boston proved useful in low level attacks against ground targets, a role the USAAF had already given its A-20 units in the Pacific. Even initially intended to be used in the traditional light bomber role as the Boston was in North Africa and Europe, 22's Bostons were soon modified for low level attacks and received four 0.50-in calibre machine guns in the nose which, added to the four existing 0.303-in guns, to make the aircraft true strafers better adapted to targets in the Pacific which were pinpoints, not area targets. Deployed in New Guinea, the RAAF Bostons suffered high attrition that reached a point, in the middle of 1943, that placed the future of the type's Australian service in jeopardy. The RAAF eventually obtained nine brand new A-20Cs from the US, delivered under the Lend-Lease Act, which were taken on charge between September and November 1943. They received the serials **A28-23 to A28-31**. The A-20Cs delivered to the RAAF were part of the P-70 program where approximately fifty A-20Cs were earmarked for P-70A-1 night fighter conversions. Thirty-nine aircraft were converted and nine surplus examples were made available to the RAAF. These aircraft were unique in that they had five 0.50-in calibre machine guns in the nose: two where the four 0.30-in calibre guns were usually placed in the cheek positions without blisters, and three mounted above the bomb aimer's glass (not a solid gun nose). Also, a strike camera was mounted behind the bomb aimer's glass, long range tanks were fitted and single 0.50-in machine guns could be found in the upper and lower gunner's positions instead of the usual twin 0.30-in and single 0.30-in respectively. At the same time, the Fifth Air Force handed over nine more A-20As that became **A28-32 to A28-40**. While the A-20Cs were used intensively by 22 Squadron, the A-20A, being more battle weary, would essentially be used for conversion training. Attrition remained high in 1943 and the first half of 1944, so the squadron soon had to face a lack of aircraft that could hamper its operational efficiency. The USAAF in the Pacific had just introduced a number of A-20Gs, so it was easy for the US to divert enough of them to re-equip 22 Squadron. All in all, and under Lend-Lease, the RAAF took charge of 29 A-20Gs that received the serials **A28-50 to A28-78**. The serials A28-41 to A28-49 was not allocated. The deliveries took place between June and October 1944. When the decision was made to re-equip the squadron with the Beaufighter after the damaging raid of 22/23 November 1944, the remainder of the serviceable A-20Gs were returned to the USAAF in the following weeks. The surviving A-20Cs were not wanted, nor the A-20As, so all were converted to components and scrapped. As the Boston III was not legally US property, the survivors did not need to be returned, but the variant encountered the same fate as most of the other A-20s.

The main US version of the A-20 was the G-model that was specifically designed with the ground support mission in mind. The bombardier's seat in the nose was removed to fit four 0.50-in calibre heavy machine guns (some early variants even had four 20mm cannons). With two more 0.50-in guns located in the lower part of the nose, the A-20G was a very effective strafer. It was widely used in Europe and the Pacific and was provided to the Soviet Union in great numbers. Here, an A-20G-35 (43-9919) is seen in the US with an extra belly tank ready for a long ferry flight.

Close-up of the nose of a A-20G in the Pacific dipslaying the six 0.50-in MGs. This concentration of this very efficient heavy machine-gun gave to the A-20G a great power of destruction.

Number of sorties: *ca. 1,400*

First operational sortie:
17.05.42
Last operational sortie:
06.12.44

Number of claims: *nil*

Total aircraft written-off: 35

Aircraft lost on operations: 27
Aircraft lost in accidents: 8

Squadron code letters:
DU

COMMANDING OFFICERS

S/L Russel E. Bell	Aus. 268	RAAF	22.04.42	07.12.42
W/C Keith McD. Hampshire	Aus. 147	RAAF	07.12.42	21.06.43
W/C Charles C. Learmonth	Aus. 385	RAAF	21.06.43	13.10.43
W/C William E. Townsend	Aus. 170	RAAF	13.10.43	04.11.43
W/C James G. Emerton *(†)*	Aus. 250283	RAAF	04.11.43	30.01.44
W/C John Hickey	Aus. 270542	RAAF	31.01.44	25.08.44
W/C Colin E. Woodman	Aus. 169	RAAF	25.08.44	...

SQUADRON USAGE

Number of 22 Squadron was originally formed at Richmond, New South Wales, in April 1936 and was given the name of 'City of Sydney' the following July. At the outbreak of war, the squadron was equipped with Avro Ansons and Hawker Demons and by December 1941 had been re-equipped with CAC Wirraways while still based at Richmond. That situation didn't change until the first Bostons arrived (A28-1, 2, 3 and 4) on 25 April 1942. Three days previously, a new CO, F/L R.E. Bell, who had arrived on the 20th, took command. On the 26th, Bostons A28-6, 7, 8 and 9 were flown from Laverton to Richmond with A28-5 following on the 30th.

The squadron was occupied with training in May, but, faced with the urgency of Australia caught in a panic due to the threat of invasion, the Bostons were rushed into anti-submarine patrols, starting on 17 May, while the conversion course was still underway. Ten patrols were carried out in May, but on 19 May A28-2 crashed on take off. The cause of the accident was simply insufficient training

A regular Air Force officer, Keith Hampshire was already at the head of a RAAF squadron, No. 6, flying Hudsons when war broke out in Asia in December 1941. He then took command of No. 23 Squadron RAAF to continue flying Hudsons. So, when he took over 22 Sqn in December 1942, Hampshire was already a very experienced leader. He led 22 during its initial steps in New Guinea and his fine leadership was eventually rewarded with a DSO. After the end of his tenure, he was posted to the UK and would become the OC of No. 456 (RAAF) Squadron, the sole RAAF night fighter unit. When he left the Mosquito-equipped 456, he had added a Bar to his DSO and a DFC.

A photo showing three Bostons flying in close formation over the Bismarck Sea at the end of 1942. The aircraft are only wearing an individual letter, typical of that early stage of the New Guinea campaign. Note the noses have been modified with extra machine guns added. The window areas were replaced with aluminium panels. In the foreground is A28-16, coded 'R', A28-15/Q (obscured) and the Boston coded 'F' is A28-5.

on the type. The pilot, F/O R.F. Fethers, was uninjured, as was the rest of the crew, and the Boston was converted to components in October. It was a bad run of luck for the squadron as another Boston (A28-17) had been lost the previous day following an engine fire during run-up. In June, the number of patrols increased to 36 and on 6 June A28-12 (F/L V.W. Morgan) was credited with the sinking of one Japanese submarine. Three days later, it was the turn of A28-3 (F/O J.C. Miles) to be credited similarly, but no Japanese submarines were sunk or even damaged in the area and these hasty confirmations had probably more to do with trying to boost morale in Australia than recording accurate data. Actually, nobody really knows what the crews saw and attacked other than the sightings possibly being of whales. In July, the anti-submarine patrols continued with most lasting three hours. On 1 August, another submarine attack took place with Sgt G.T. Smith (A28-18) causing possible damage to a target attacked 15 miles off Tuggerah. Otherwise, there was no change in the mission given to 22, but the serviceability of the Bostons was fairly poor that month with an average of just five aircraft available daily. Despite this, the squadron logged 515 hours of training and operational flying.

After 170 anti-submarine patrols, a major change occurred in the squadron's life when, on 4 September, it began the move to Port Moresby. By 5 November, it was established at Ward's Strip a few miles north of Moresby. The move was not without incident, however, as A28-19 crashed on 9 October (the crew were uninjured). Some practice flights were also carried out, but, unfortunately, one ended tragically for A28-12 when, on 11 November, it blew up during a bombing training sortie.

The moment of truth came on 15 November when three Bostons were dispatched for an armed reconnaissance on a coastal area - A28-21 (S/L Bell), A28-14 (F/L C.R. Sladen), and A28-20 (F/L K.R. McDonald). This operational flight was short, just half an hour, and all three aircraft returned to base with nothing to report. The following day, the Bostons had the opportunity to use their offensive weapons when they attacked barges during another armed reconnaissance led by F/L McDonald. Six aircraft were airborne that day in two elements of three and even though the barges appeared unserviceable, one was destroyed and eight more hit while the stern of a wreck was also hit. One anti-aircraft position at Giruwa was also silenced. After five days without operations, enemy troop concentrations were attacked on the 21st. The next day over Buna strip, A28-22 blew up while on the bombing run and A28-20 suffered a similar fate three days later while attacking enemy ground positions. There were no survivors and the squadron had experienced a very bad start with the loss of two Bostons in nineteen sorties. In December, the number of sorties increased, 49 sorties across nine effective operations. A change of command took place on the 7th when S/L K.M. Hampshire, a very experienced pilot, took over. At the same time, the squadron had really started to settle in to its role. No losses were reported that month.

There was no time to celebrate the New Year and on 1 January 1943 three Bostons, led by S/L Hampshire, bombed and strafed Salamaua township and the Sanananda area followed by a reconnaissance to the Ambuga River. The three Bostons returned to base after three hours and ten minutes flying. Two more ops involving a section were flown on the 2nd and the 4th. On the 7th, six Bostons were dispatched to bomb and strafe grounded aircraft at Lae. One Boston, A28-7, had to return early owing to a faulty air-speed indicator, but the five remaining aircraft completed the op. Over the target, A28-4, flown by F/O R.A. Wines, was hit by flak, rendering the hydraulics unserviceable, and the Boston crash-landed at Jackson Field with no injuries to the crew. The aircraft, however, was a write-off. The squadron would operate for another thirteen days until the end of January without incident and flew 72 sorties (204 operational hours), dropped eighty 250-lb and eighty 500-lbs bombs, and fired 83,400 rounds of ammunition for the month. In February, the unit continued to support Allied ground forces that were facing another Japanese offensive. However, the squadron only flew 55 sorties, in ten days of operations in February, with all being armed reconnaissance flights. On the 6th, A28-21 was seen on fire near Lapur Point, and crashed into the sea three hundred yards off shore and two miles north of Knirps Island, after attacking Garrison Hill. It is believed that it had been shot down by ground fire; all on board were killed. On the next raid, on the 9th, it was the turn of A28-14 which failed to return after it disappeared from the returning formation in bad weather. It was last seen entering cloud at 16,500 feet with the rest of the formation, but did not emerge on the other side. The crew was posted as missing. The busiest day was the 22nd when two ops were flown. The morning flight consisted of seven aircraft led by W/C Hampshire with four more Bostons led by S/L C.C. Learmonth dispatched in the afternoon. The squadron maintained the pressure in March and 73 sorties were carried out in fourteen operations. The first raid was mounted on the 2nd with an attack on Lae aerodrome by six Bostons led by W/C Hampshire. The attack was repeated the following day, but S/L Learmonth, who was leading the op, failed to take off due to engine trouble so F/L W.E. Newton assumed command. Learmonth was able to lead an afternoon strike by five Bostons on a Japanese convoy. This attack was flown in conjunction with other Allied aircraft (The Battle of the Bismarck Sea). Two direct hits (250-lb bombs) were scored on a destroyer just forward of midships. The convoy was, however, escorted by fighters and A28-7 (F/O H.B. Craig) was attacked by one 'Zeke', but the latter broke away after being fired upon. Another 'Zeke' made a frontal attack on A28-6 (F/O A.N. Skinner) at approximately 1500 feet, but the Boston dived towards the water and the Japanese pilot broke away. Four more 'Zekes' commenced individual attacks on A28-7 from the rear, but F/O Craig turned into them and fired short bursts until they broke away. Boston A28-13 (F/O R.A. Wines) was also attacked, but the Japanese fighters did not press home their attacks. The combined actions by Beaufighters, B-17s and B-25s, in addition to the Bostons, provided too many targets to take care of. One of the two Japanese destroyers, *Shirayuki* would eventually sink from the combined attack of the Australians and Americans. The squadron returned to normal operations for the next three days then none were carried out between the 7th and the 15th. On the 16th, seven Bostons led by the CO were airborne at around 08.00 and heading for Salamaua to attacks stores and buildings on the foreshore. Heavy flak was encountered but, despite this, the raid was considered successful and large fires were started in the target area. During the action, F/L 'Bill' Newton, who was piloting A28-7, displayed distinguished valour in continuing his attack despite having received four direct hits that caused the loss of one engine and substantial damage to the wings, fuselage, systems, control surfaces and fuel tanks. Nevertheless, he led the attack and delivered his bombs from low altitude. Newton managed to return to base, a long 180 miles, with his badly damaged Boston. Two days later, six more Bostons retur-

Number 22 Squadron Bostons and A-20Cs forming up over Kiriwina Island for strike on New Britain (Gogosi-Kiava and Bialla Plantations). The aircraft are now wearing the squadron code 'DU'. Seen in this image are: A28-18/DU-Y, A28-25/DU-N, A28-5/DU-F, A28-9/DU-K, A28-30/DU-W, A28-28/DU-U, A28-27/DU-H and A28-10/DU-L. *(AHM & WA)*.

Two images showing how the Bostons were used in action: flying very low and very vulnerable to ground fire. Below, A28-5/DU-F has its bomb bay doors open and has just released its deadly load (see the bomb at the bottom of the image) while on strike on Cape Hoskins Strip, New Britain. The other Bostons identified are A28-24/DU-P, A28-23/DU-O, A28-11/DU-M, A28-28/DU-U, A28-30/DU-W and A28-6/DU-G (forefront on the image above). The photo was taken on 21 December 1943 when 22 was using a mixed force of Bostons and A-20Cs. *(AHM & WA)*.

William Newton, from the state of Victoria, who would become the RAAF's only Victoria Cross recipient of the Pacific war, enlisted as an air cadet in February 1940. When the hostilities against Japan began in December 1941, he had been serving as a flying instructor for about a year. With the situation in Asia worsening, he left this position and undertook a conversion course on the Hudson and was posted to No. 22 Squadron in May 1942, as it was about to convert to the Boston, with the rank of Flight Lieutenant.

ned to the same target to complete the job, F/L Newton and his crew now flying A28-3. The attack was also successful and he scored a direct hit on the buildings while under intense AA fire. A28-3 was seen leaving the area with smoke pouring from it and was soon seen to catch fire. The Boston made an emergency landing one and a half miles out to sea and sank in a few seconds. Sergeant Basil G. Eastwood, the navigator, did not survive the crash, but Newton and Sgt John Lyons did. They managed to swim to shore where they were soon captured. They were interrogated until the 20th before being moved to Lae where Lyon was bayoneted to death on the orders of Rear Admiral Ruitaro Fujita, the senior Japanese commander in the area. As for Newton, he was brought back to Salamaua where, on 29 March, he was ceremonially beheaded with a Samurai sword by the naval officer who had captured him. The squadron knew nothing of the fate of the crew until the following September when Salamaua was recaptured and Newton's body found. When positive identification of Newton's remains was established, he was posthumously awarded the Victoria Cross on 19 October. The citation reads:

'Flight Lieutenant Newton served with No. 22 Squadron, Royal Australian Air Force, in New Guinea from May, 1942, to March, 1943, and completed 52 operational sorties. Throughout, he displayed great courage and an iron determination to inflict the utmost damage on the enemy. His splendid offensive flying and fighting were attended with brilliant success. Disdaining evasive tactics when under the heaviest fire, he always went straight to his objectives. He carried out many daring machine-gun attacks on enemy positions involving low-flying over long distances in the face of continuous fire at point-blank range. On three occasions, he dived through intense anti-aircraft fire to release his bombs on important targets on the Salamaua Isthmus. On one of these occasions, his starboard engine failed over the target, but he succeeded in flying back to an airfield 160 miles away. When leading an attack on an objective on 16th March, 1943, he dived through intense and accurate shell fire and his aircraft was hit repeatedly. Nevertheless, he held to his course and bombed his target from a low level. The attack resulted in the destruction of many buildings and dumps, including two 40,000-gallon fuel installations. Although his aircraft was crippled, with fuselage and wing sections torn, petrol tanks pierced, mainplanes and engines seriously damaged, and one of the main tires flat, Flight Lieutenant Newton managed to fly it back to base and make a successful landing. Despite this harassing experience, he returned next day to the same locality. His target, this time a single building, was even more difficult but he again attacked with his usual courage and resolution, flying a steady course through a barrage of fire. He scored a hit on the building but at the same moment his aircraft burst into flames. Flight Lieutenant Newton maintained control and calmly turned his aircraft away and flew along the shore. He saw it as his duty to keep the aircraft in the air as long as he could so as to take his crew as far away as possible from the enemy's positions. With great skill, he brought his blazing aircraft down on the water. Two members of the crew were able to extricate themselves and were seen swimming to the shore, but the gallant pilot is missing. According to other air crews who witnessed the occurrence, his escape-hatch was not opened and his dinghy was not inflated. Without regard to his own safety, he had done all that man could do to prevent his crew from falling into enemy hands. Flight Lieutenant Newton's many examples of conspicuous bravery have rarely been equaled and will serve as a shining inspiration to all who follow him.'

Newton became the only Australian airman to earn the decoration in the South West Pacific theatre of World War II, and the only one while flying with an RAAF squadron. In the meantime, 22 Squadron continued its mission and by the end of March more than thirty sorties had been flown in six operations. The same intensity was maintained in April, May and June without the loss of any aircraft over more than 150 sorties. However on 24 May, the squadron recorded the death of Arthur C.H. Taylor, the lower gunner of A28-8 flown by F/O H.M. Rowell. Sadly, Taylor received a direct shell hit from below which decapitated him. The top gunner, Sgt David O. Duncan, was also hit by shrapnel and had to have his right foot partially amputated on return to base. The squadron also lost a Boston during a flight test on 1 June when the aircraft, A28-13, dived into a glassy smooth sea while testing the front guns and sight. All four on board - F/L P.C. Mullens, F/Sgt M.J. Collins, Sgt N.H. Sail (mechanic) and LAC J.J. Moore (armourer) - perished. Other than S/L Learmonth taking command of the squadron from W/C Hampshire, who was posted to RAAF HQ on 1 August, no major changes

occurred in July and August, the squadron continuing its support missions, with an average of six Bostons supplied for every operation. The targets included barges, troops concentrations and other facilities. On 29 August, the squadron came close to losing more Bostons while carrying out another barge sweep. The Japanese had so far been relatively inaccurate, but this time, of the six aircraft detailed for the op, three were badly damaged. A28-9 (F/O A.C. Young) had its hydraulics shot out, and returned with various holes in the fuselage, tail and fin as well as the left flap. Unable to lower the undercarriage, Young made a belly landing. The Boston was later repaired. Bostons A28-5 (F/O H.P. Gunson) and A28-11 (F/L C.R. Sladen) returned with holes in various locations and Sladen was badly injured by a piece of shrapnel that lodged itself deep in his body. He suffered considerable pain and loss of blood, but managed to return to base. At the end of the month, the squadron moved to Vivigani Strip on Goodenough Island and operations resumed as early as 4 September with a morning bombing raid on Gasmata Strip by three Bostons led by F/O A.N. Skinner. In the afternoon, the attack was repeated, but led by F/O H.M. Rowell. This target would remain the focus for the next few days, but on the 10th and the 11th the squadron was occupied with searching for a missing Beaufighter of the Wing (22 Squadron, with the Beaufighters of 30 Squadron, was part of 77 Wing). Offensive ops resumed on the 12th with another typical barge sweep on Alau Passage and Awul on Gasmata Island, but the operation turned into a disaster. Boston A28-15 (F/L H.B. Dawkins, leading the formation) was hit in one engine by ground fire and was forced to ditch. All three crew members were seen in their dinghy soon after, but that would be the last time they were seen. Semple perished while Dawkins and Thomas were taken prisoner and died in captivity on 22 July 1944 and 5 May 1944 respectively. Another Boston was posted missing, A28-16 crewed by F/Sgt E.G.T. Riley and F/Sgt L.K. Wilson, was last seen leaving the target. Boston A28-8 (F/O H.M. Rowell) was not in good shape either, having many holes in the cockpit and forward fuselage, causing a hydraulic failure, but Rowell managed to return to base. At first the landing gear refused to lower and it was only after a series of manoeuvers that he could get his wheels fully extended, but not his flaps. The landing was correctly executed, but without flaps or brakes, the Boston rolled off the runway and was badly damaged in the ensuing crash. The ground crew estimated that Rowell had been down to his last five minutes of petrol. This Boston was too damaged and would later be converted to components. With these losses and about half a dozen Bostons temporarily out of action, the squadron was only able to field three aircraft for the op on the 21st.

The replacement A-20Cs supplied by the Americans arrived at the squadron towards the end of September with eight being taken on charge. Training was carried out on the aircraft. A28-26 met a brutal end when it was lost on 11 October after it crashed on take-off for a practice bombing sortie. The nose-wheel strut folded up and the A-20 slid along the strip and overturned in a shallow ditch at the end of the strip where it caught fire and the bombs exploded. As the escape hatch was above the cockpit and sitting on the ground, nothing could be done for the pilot, F/O J.B. Knight, but, thankfully, F/Sgt K.G. Thompson survived, severely shocked, and LAC R.F. McCabe, a mechanic and passenger for this flight, was slightly injured. No operations were carried out until 19 October when two A-20Cs, led by W/C W.E. Townsend (A28-23), the new CO since 1 October, conducted a barge sweep. The other pilot was F/O A.C. Young (A28-24). In the afternoon, two more sorties were flown by Boston IIIs. Until the end of the month the squadron continued its attacks against barges and 25 sorties were flown. Barges remained the main target in November, but, on the 3rd, the squadron was requested to bomb the Palmalmal plantations. Five A-20Cs, led by the CO, were dispatched for the task. All bombs were dropped and were seen to explode, but A28-29, flown by the CO, was hit by ground fire and compelled to ditch in the waters of Jacquinot Bay. The crew was posted missing, but actually survived and would turn up one month later. Two days later, the squadron came close to losing another Boston when A28-25 was severely damaged after the second of two 250-lb bombs exploded prematurely beneath the aircraft. Luckily both engines continued to function normally to return the Boston and its crew to base. The aircraft was sent for repairs, but would never return to the squadron. In the meantime, W/C J. Emerton had arrived the previous day to take command. The same plantation was attacked on the 4th and, after an attack on buildings and shore installations at Ubili and Ulamona the next day, the squadron returned to its barge sweeps until the end of the month when a bombing op on Garove Island was performed in conjunction with the Beaufighters of 30 Squadron. In the meantime, from the 16th, the squadron had moved to Kiriwina. In December, the number of sorties increased steadily even though the commitment of aircraft to each op remained small (two or three). On the 21st, however, a bombing raid on Cape Hoskins, led by the CO, was carried out with seven aircraft. The squadron flew operations on 21 days in January 1944, but remained under utilised. Close to sixty sorties were flown and, if we ignore a handful of supply dropping sorties (on the 18th and the 19th) and a handful of photo reconnaissance sorties, the main task remained barge sweeps on the north and south coasts of New Britain. Japanese flak was not very active nor very accurate, but some hits were recorded on a few Bostons, like A28-5 and A28-10 which returned from their op on the 23rd with four and two hits (none serious) respectively. The next day, it was the turn of A28-6 to be hit and the pilot,

F/O C.J. Sugden, made a crash landing back at base, with a wounded F/Sgt H.W.R. Hughes, the wireless operator, on board. The Boston was repaired and would return to service with the squadron in June. However, the Japanese anti-aircraft fire was very accurate on the 30th when it hit A28-27 during another barge sweep. Flown by the CO himself, it was flying with another A-20C (A28-30 flown by F/O M.J. Carse) when it was seen to burst into flames and crash approximatively 300 yards from a gun position on the Kabu River. There was no chance for Emerton or his wireless operator, P/O T.J. Gawne, to survive. Despite no operations being flown during the first ten days of February, the squadron carried out close to seventy sorties that month. Command was temporarily given to S/L J. Hickey, one of the two flight commanders. Operations remained unchanged with, as for January, some photo-reconnaissance sorties also flown. During one such sortie on the 29th, A28-28 (F/O C.J. Sugden) encountered trouble with its starboard engine close to base, and soon the aircraft was uncontrollable, losing height rapidly from 8000 feet to 4000 feet. The rear gunner, F/O R.O. Whitford bailed out at 3000 feet on orders from the captain. Sugden was ready to do likewise and jettisoned the hatch, but changed his mind and managed, with a huge effort, to regain control and land safely. Whitford's parachute opened normally and he landed in the water. Sugden had managed to report Whitford's predicament and an ASR flight, consisting of three aircraft from the squadron, took off to search (and were joined by aircraft from 76 and 30 Squadrons). Whitford was soon located and was eventually picked up by a Dornier flying boat soon after. In March, after a halt of a few days, operations resumed. An aircraft was lost on the 17th when A28-24 was posted missing after a barge attack. It was seen to ditch about 30 miles from base due to petrol shortage. The engines had cut out at 1200 feet. Fortunately, the two crewmembers, F/L D.N. Daly and P/O J.W. Hill, were later rescued by a Dornier 24 (A49-1). Otherwise, two main operations were mounted against plantations on the 24th and the 25th, with eight and six aircraft launched respectively. Both were led by W/C Hickey who had been confirmed in command and promoted since then.

In April, with the landing of the Americans at Talasea, Cape Hoskins, and the capture of Hoskins Strip and the Ubili garrison on the north coast of New Britain, and along with the landing on the south coast of Arawe and the subsequent capture of Gasmata Strip, the New Britain campaign, as far as 22 Squadron was concerned, was virtually over and only fourteen sorties were logged that month. In May, the squadron was stood down and took the opportunity to rest and reform as, during the month, it was notified that an allotment of twelve Douglas A-20Gs would be received in June. The timing was perfect as the squadron was once again down to ten operational

As the attrition of the Bostons was high, the US helped the Australians by supplying several A-20Cs as replacements. The A-20C was the improved American version of the British Boston. Like the Bostons, the A-20Cs were modified in due course as strafers with extra machine guns mounted in the nose.

Wing Commander J. Emerton, on the left, is seen with war photographer Frank Bagnel and Flying Officer T. Gawne, Emerton's gunner. Emerton and Gawne were killed in action a couple of weeks later on 31 January 1944. *(AHM & WA)*

aircraft. Training on the type occurred during June as the squadron began preparations to move again. Nevertheless, 22 was called to carry out an op on the 24th (A28-11, A28-30 and A28-34 took off at one hour intervals) in conjunction with six P-40s of No. 77 Squadron. This operation was to cover the withdrawal of HMS *Vendetta* from Waterfall Bay. The squadron packed up and arrived at their new base, Noemfoor, on 10 July, with the A-20s arriving in the days that followed - eleven on the 11th and six on the 12th. There, training resumed and continued until mid-August. The new A-20Gs had their baptism of fire on the 15th when eight (A28-50, 51, 52, 55, 56, 58, 60 and 64) were detailed to undertake a barge sweep. The raid was led by S/L C.E. Woodman who took command from W/C Hickey ten days later. Now, compared to the previous months, the squadron operated with greater intensity, flying 110 sorties in the second fortnight of August during which 112 500-lb bombs, 127 250-lb bombs and 100 100-lb bombs were dropped. There was also close to 60,000 .50-in and 2,000 .30-in rounds fired. The squadron mainly flew the A-20Gs, but the earlier aircraft were still operational as twenty sorties were flown by Boston IIIs or A-20Cs that month. No operational loss was reported, but one A-20C (A28-30) was damaged on the 21st when an accidental discharge of a gun occurred. The aircraft was sent for repairs that were never undertaken and was struck off charge and converted to components in February 1945. One A-20G (A28-56) had a short career with the RAAF when, on returning from an op on the 17th, it crash-landed at base due to hydraulic failure. The crew was uninjured and the aircraft was sent to a repair facility before it was handed back to the Americans in March 1945.

September continued August's activity with a record 112 sorties flown. All sorties were flown by A-20Gs with the other earlier variants now relegated to training or other tasks. However, this record left a bitter taste as eleven crew members were posted 'missing believed killed' and no less than six A-20Gs were written-off. The first was A28-63 (F/O D. McKenzie, a Kiwi serving in the RAAF) which was hit by ground fire in the left nacelle and the fuselage from turret to tail. The brakes were damaged and failed on landing when returning from a strike on the 5th and the aircraft hit a moving truck. The crew escaped injury, but the A-20G was a total wreck. Two weeks later, six A-20Gs were detailed for a strike on Boela strip during which twenty bombs were dropped with sixteen seen exploding on the strip itself. The op was considered as very successful, but A28-53 did not return and the crew, P/O H.L. Atkins and P/O R.E. Gehrman, were lost. The aircraft was seen plunging into trees during recovery from a strafing run. This loss began a bad sequence for the squadron. Four days later, during a barge sweep, A28-55 was seen crashing into the sea one mile off shore between Elaar and Danar, presumably after being hit by flak. The cockpit was on fire and the pilot (F/L G.I. Murrie) jumped from 300 feet, but, sadly, his chute did not open and he was seen to hit the water. The A-20G sank in a couple of seconds. Two days later, A28-50 would be lost in the same circumstances during another barge sweep. Both crews were killed. Bad luck had certainly found the squadron this month and, to make things worse, one A-20G was lost in an accident. The aircraft, A28-61, flown by F/O J.E. Davidson, had been detailed for a test flight at 16.30 on the 14th and was seen taking-off with no indication of a problem. It never returned to base. A corvette reported the aircraft had crashed half an hour after its departure from the airfield. Searches were launched that day and the following day, but no trace of the personnel on board (Davidson had taken a navigator and three LACs with him) was found, nor was any explanation for the crash forthcoming. In October, the squadron faced a lack of crews as those missing were not immediately replaced, and the situation was aggravated with leave periods and other postings. Therefore, the squadron completed less sorties (90) that month. However, no operational losses were sustained even though some aircraft were damaged by ground fire. A28-52, for example, was obliged to return on one engine, after being hit on the 4th, and landed at Sansapor with less than 20 gallons of fuel! Before the end of the month, three other A-20Gs sustained damage from AA to various degrees, but all without major consequences for the aircraft or crew. Little activity was recorded in November because the Allies had achieved their objectives. One photo-reconnaissance op, which involved four A-20Gs, was flown

When 22 moved to Morotai Island in late 1944, a couple of older A-20Cs were still on charge, like A28-28/DU-U. It was used for training purposes within the squadron. It survived the 22 November 1944 raid and was returned to operational condition, flying one more op on 1 December. Not wanted by the Americans, who were no longer using the C-model in combat, it was stored and converted to components in February 1945. *(AHM & WA)*

before the squadron moved to Morotai (now in Allied hands and where a major base was established) on the 17th. Operations resumed the next day in support of the US landings in the Philippines with eight A-20Gs detailed to attack Sidate Drome. Sixteen bombs exploded on the strip, eight more in the revetment area and two coastal schooners were attacked and claimed as probably destroyed. Two more ops involving eight A-20Gs were flown on the 20th and the 22nd with all aircraft returning safely to base. The airfield was attacked by Japanese aircraft during the night and A28-51, 52, 60 and 67 were totally destroyed. A28-6, 10, 59, 68, 75 and 76 sustained serious damage that required repairs at an RSU, and A28-54, and 57 were also damaged, but repairable on site within seven days. Boston A28-6 was to be declared beyond economical repair and struck off charge two weeks later, while A28-10, 59, 68, 75 and 76, while apparently repairable, were converted to components at the end of April 1945 (the final decision is believed to have been freezed until that date). Out of action for a short while, the squadron resumed normal operations at the end of the month with half of the usual number of aircraft as earlier ops (four A-20Gs). Operations continued until 6 December when the last operation with A-20Gs was carried out. Four aircraft (A28-62, 66, 77 and 78) attacked the powerhouse at Manao in the Philippines. The following day the whole squadron returned to Noemfoor to be re-equipped with Beaufighters. The decision to give up the A-20G was mainly due to the fact that 22 was the only RAAF unit to fly the type, a type that had been supplied via Lend-Lease and carried with it the requisite financial consequences at war's end. The night raid that decimated the squadron's strength was a good opportunity to stop asking the Americans for material as the Beaufighter was produced in Australia. All A-20s were soon returned to the USAAF, at least the ones they wanted, like the A-20G, and all of the remaining earlier marks were finally converted to components during the first weeks of 1945. For 22 Squadron, it was a return to some sort of normality as the Boston/A-20 had been a bit of an oddity, albeit a useful one, in the RAAF for about two and a half years.

Taken on 29 October 1944 on Oemfoor Island in the Dutch Guinea, this photo give the atmosphere of the 22 while in operations. While one Douglas A-20G is being re-armed with bombs by ground crew, crews who are taking part in the next sortie are preparing the navigation. from left to right, Warrant Officer L.C. Fanning, pilot, Sergeant R. Cameron, navigator, Flight Lieutenant C.E. Spence, pilot and Flying Officer G.T. Dick, navigator.

Date	Crew	S/N	Origin	Serial	Code	Fate
26.11.42	F/L Kenneth R. **McDonald**	Aus. 250430	RAAF	**A28-22**	Y	†
	F/O Thomas E. **O'Neill**	Aus. 407451	RAAF			†
	Sgt Charles R. **Napier**	Aus. 420247	RAAF			†
29.11.42	F/O Herbert J. **Bullmore**	Aus. 402045	RAAF	**A28-20**	W	†
	Sgt John W. **McKay**	Aus. 405492	RAAF			†
	Sgt Ian C. **Stodart**	Aus. 413801	RAAF			†
07.01.43	F/O Robert A. **Wines**	Aus. 402432	RAAF	**A28-4**	F	-
	Sgt Clifford **Grove**	Aus. 411020	RAAF			-
	Sgt Harry **Jamieson**	Aus. 420007	RAAF			-
06.02.43	P/O George T. **Smith**	Aus. 401793	RAAF	**A28-21**	X	†
	Sgt Roderick T. **Kerr**	Aus. 401799	RAAF			†
	Sgt Lance **Dawes**	Aus. 414541	RAAF			†
09.02.43	F/O Lesland A. **Kenway**	Aus. 405590	RAAF	**A28-14**	P	†
	F/Sgt Francis C. **Gordon**	Aus. 405047	RAAF			†
	Sgt Horace W. **Hall**	Aus. 414486	RAAF			†
18.03.43	F/L William E. **Newton***	Aus. 250748	RAAF	**A28-3**	Y	†
	Sgt John **Lyon***	Aus. 401706	RAAF			†
	Sgt Basil G. **Eastwood**	Aus. 13055	RAAF			†
12.09.43	F/O Harold M. **Rowell**	Aus. 406958	RAAF	**A28-8**	DU-J	-
	F/Sgt Douglas F. **Lyons**	Aus. 420018	RAAF			-
	F/Sgt Harry **Jamieson**	Aus. 420007	RAAF			-

Boston A28-8 seen shortly after its crash-landing on Vivigani strip (Goodenough Island) on 12 September 1943. Fortunately, the crew escaped unharmed.

Date	Name	Service No.	Air Force	Aircraft	Code	
	F/L Harry B. **Dawkins***	Aus. 280791	RAAF	**A28-15**	DU-Q	†
	Sgt Douglas G. **Semple**	Aus. 26741	RAAF			†
	Sgt Gordon R. **Thomas***	Aus. 417011	RAAF			†
	F/Sgt Eric G.T. **Riley**	Aus. 411522	RAAF	**A28-16**	DU-R	†
	Sgt Lindsay K. **Wilson**	Aus. 413921	RAAF			†
03.11.43	W/C William E. **Townsend**	Aus. 170	RAAF	**A28-29**		-
	F/O David M. **McClymont**	Aus. 405491	RAAF			-
30.01.44	W/C James G. **Emerton**	Aus. 250283	RAAF	**A28-27**		†
	P/O Terence J. **Gawne**	Aus. 408648	RAAF			†
17.03.44	F/L David N. **Daly**	Aus. 260707	RAAF	**A28-24**	DU-P	-
	P/O John W. **Hill**	Aus. 419649	RAAF			-
05.09.44	F/O Dargan **McKenzie**	Aus. 402802	(nz)/RAAF	**A28-63**	DU-T	-
	F/Sgt Reginald E. **Pedlow**	Aus. 37653	RAAF			-
20.09.44	P/O Henry L. **Atkins**	Aus. 419377	RAAF	**A28-53**	DU-D	†
	P/O Ronald E. **Gehrman**	Aus. 43071	RAAF			†
23.09.44	F/L Glen I. **Murrie**	Aus. 416600	RAAF	**A28-55**	DU-F	†
	F/O George I. **Rowlands**	Aus. 425223	RAAF			†
25.09.44	F/O John E. **Warren**	Aus. 402424	RAAF	**A28-50**	DU-A	†
	P/O Kenneth E. **Clark**	Aus. 435163	RAAF			†
22.11.44	*Damaged in air raid*	-	-	**A28-6**		-
	Damaged in air raid	-	-	**A28-10**	DU-L	-
	Destroyed in air raid	-	-	**A28-51**	DU-B	-
	Destroyed in air raid	-	-	**A28-52**	DU-C	-
	Damaged in air raid	-	-	**A28-59**	DU-M	-
	Destroyed in air raid	-	-	**A28-60**	DU-P	-
	Damaged in air raid	-	-	**A28-65**	DU-G	-
	Destroyed in air raid	-	-	**A28-67**	DU-V	-
	Damaged in air raid	-	-	**A28-68**	DU-X	-
	Damaged in air raid	-	-	**A28-75**	DU-A	-
	Damaged in air raid	-	-	**A28-76**		-

Total: 27

**Died in captivity.*

A scene of destruction after the night Japanese raid of 22 November 1944. Here the remains of some RAAF Bostons and A-20Gs can be seen. The raid damaged thirteen of the squadron's aircraft, five being either destroyed or damaged beyond economical repair. This marked the end of Boston/A-20 usage in the RAAF.

Date	Crew	S/N	Origin	Serial	Code	Fate
18.05.42	*ground accident*	-	-	**A28-17**	-	-
09.10.42	Sgt Warwick **ADDISON**	Aus. 405707	RAAF	**A28-19**		-
	rest of the crew if any, not known.					
10.11.42	F/L Vernon W. **MORGAN**	Aus. 250550	RAAF	**A28-12**	-	†
	P/O John H. **BORLAND**	Aus. 405569	RAAF			†
	Sgt Ronald T. **POWER**	Aus. 420053	RAAF			†
01.06.43	F/L Philip C. **MULLENS**	Aus. 402249	RAAF	**A28-13**	O	†
	F/Sgt Austin J. **COLLINS**	Aus. 400871	RAAF			†
	Sgt Norman H. **SAILL***	Aus. 33313	RAAF			†
	LAC John E. **MOORE***	Aus. 20932	RAAF			†
11.10.43	F/O James B. **KNIGHT**	Aus. 19067	RAAF	**A28-26**		†
	F/Sgt Keith G. **THOMPSON**	Aus. 420078	RAAF			-
	LAC Richard F. **McGLADE**	Aus. 13731	RAAF			-
17.06.44	P/O Jack **BOSTELMAN**	Aus. 406635	RAAF	**A28-7**	DU-H	-
	F/Sgt James A. **WOOD**	Aus. 422786	RAAF			-
04.07.44	W/O Anthony C. **DOBSON**	Aus. 413972	RAAF	**A28-1**	DU-A	-
	F/Sgt Kevin J. **GRACE**	Aus. 410798	RAAF			-
14.09.44	F/O James E. **DAVIDSON**	Aus. 406923	RAAF	**A28-61**		†
	W/O Wallis C. **GLEW**	Aus. 410973	RAAF			†
	LAC Charles V. **BONE***	Aus. 16961	RAAF			†
	LAC William A. **COSTIGAN***	Aus. 73200	RAAF			†
	LAC Frank **STREET***	Aus. 69438	RAAF			†

Total: 8

**passenger (mechanic)*

A front view of A28-19 after its accident on 9 October 1942. The aircraft was too damaged to consider any repair. Fortunately, the crew survived.
(AHM & WA)

(Known number of take-offs/sorties and codes when known of aircraft made available to No. 22 Sqn, the breakdown of the first missions carried out in 1942 is not known)

Did not return from its last mission

Serials and Codes (when known)	Type	Formerly	Known mission tally
A28-1 : A/DU-A	Boston III	AL890	3

Boston A28-1/A being recovered after it crashed during a night take off on 30 November 1942.
(AHM & WA)

Serials and Codes (when known)	Type	Formerly	Known mission tally
A28-2:	Boston III	AL347	1
A28-3: C	Boston III	AL887	*20
A28-4: E	Boston III	AL893	14
A28-5: F/DU-F	Boston III	AL895	76
A28-6: G/DU-G	Boston III	AL897	87
A28-7: H/DU-H	Boston III	AL899	67
A28-8: J/DU-J	Boston III	AL907	58
A28-9: K/DU-K	Boston III	AL891	81
A28-10: L/DU-L	Boston III	AL358	27
A28-11: M/DU-M	Boston III	AL364	55
A28-12:	Boston III	AL365	10
A28-13: O	Boston III	AL367	43
A28-14: P	Boston III	AL892	*32
A28-15: Q/DU-Q	Boston III	AL361	*63
A28-16: R/DU-R	Boston III	AL362	*56
A28-17:	Boston III	AL363	-
A28-18: Y/DU-Y	Boston III	AL366	33
A28-19:	Boston III	AL368	13
A28-20: W	Boston III	AL369	*7
A28-21: X	Boston III	AL894	*30
A28-22: Y	Boston III	AL898	*9
A28-23: DU-O	A-20C-5-DO	42-33154	55
A28-24: DU-P	A-20C-5-DO	42-33163	48
A28-25: DU-N	A-20C-5-DO	42-33172	29
A28-26:	A-20C-5-DO	42-33180	1
A28-27:	A-20C-5-DO	42-33134	17

A28-28: DU-U	A-20C-5-DO	42-33142	**33**
A28-29:	A-20C-10-DO	42-33211	**5**
A28-30: DU-W	A-20C-5-DO	42-33174	**45**
A28-31:	A-20C-5-DO	42-33168	-
A28-32:	A-20A-DO	40-0085	-
A28-33:	A-20A-DO	40-0143	-
A28-34: DU-B	A-20A-DO	40-3160	**1**
A28-35:	A-20A-DO	40-0162	**1**

A rare photo of a A-20A, here A28-34/DU-B flying over the Bismarck Sea. Even if they could be used in operations, the nine A-20As received were kept in reserve and used for training as they were considered as being rather battle weary. Only two operational sorties were recorded on this type including one on A28-34.
(AHM & WA)

A28-36:	A-20A-DO	40-0077	-
A28-37:	A-20A-DO	40-0118	-
A28-38:	A-20A-DO	40-0139	-
A28-39:	A-20A-DO	40-0144	-
A28-40:	A-20A-DO	40-3159	-
A28-41 to A28-49 not allocated			
A28-50: DU-A	A-20G-40-DO	43-21296	**17**
A28-51: DU-B	A-20G-40-DO	43-21306	**30**
A28-52: DU-C	A-20G-40-DO	43-21308	**21**
A28-53: DU-D	A-20G-40-DO	43-21311	**15**
A28-54: DU-E	A-20G-40-DO	43-21540	**31**
A28-55: DU-F	A-20G-40-DO	43-21303	**11**
A28-56:	A-20G-40-DO	43-21314	**4**
A28-57: DU-J	A-20G-40-DO	43-21301	**28**
A28-58: DU-K	A-20G-40-DO	43-21294	**42**
A28-59: DU-M	A-20G-40-DO	43-21542	**17**
A28-60: DU-P	A-20G-40-DO	43-21545	**21**
A28-61:	A-20G-40-DO	43-21380	**3**
A28-62: DU-S	A-20G-40-DO	43-21381	**17**
A28-63: DU-T	A-20G-40-DO	43-21384	**2**
A28-64: DU-N	A-20G-40-DO	43-21387	**7**
A28-65: DU-G	A-20G-45-DO	43-21953	**17**
A28-66: DU-H	A-20G-45-DO	43-21976	**25**
A28-67: DU-V	A-20G-45-DO	43-21977	**11**
A28-68: DU-X	A-20G-45-DO	43-21985	**16**
A28-69:	A-20G-10-DO	42-54069	-

A28-68/DU-P seen while undergoing repairs in the open after having been damaged by ground fire on 4 October 1944. Only a tarpaulin has been installed over the area under repair to protect the fitters from the burning sun of the South West Pacific. *(AHM & WA)*

A28-70:		A-20G-10-DO	42-54091	-
A28-71:		A-20G-10-DO	42-54073	-
A28-72:		A-20G-10-DO	42-54092	-
A28-73:		A-20G-10-DO	42-54098	-
A28-74:		A-20G-10-DO	42-54120	-
A28-75:	DU-A	A-20G-45-DO	43-21970	-
A28-76:		A-20G-45-DO	43-21978	2
A28-77:		A-20G-45-DO	43-22250	13
A28-78:	DU-R	A-20G-45-DO	43-22148	10

Douglas A28-63 in an uncomfortable position after being damaged by enemy action on 6 September 1944. The Havoc crashed on landing at Kamiri strip owing to brake failure and ran off the strip. While the crew escaped injury, the aircraft was eventually condemned and converted to components. Note that the aircraft is wearing the letter 'T' only, the 'DU' was blanked out by censors for unknown reasons.
(AHM & WA)

Douglas A20G A28-66 coded DU-H seen at Morotai in the autumn 1944. He would be returned to the 5th Air Force in January 1945. Note that as for serial, only a white '66' was painted under the tailplane.
(AHM & WA)

Douglas A-20G A28-78/DU-R, christened 'Topsy', seen in the autumn of 1944 at Morotai. Note that this aircraft is yet to adhere to the international regulations regarding national markings as, even though it is serving with the Australian unit, the US star and bars is still applied under the wing. The wearing of two different national markings was prohibited by the Geneva Convention. On the other hand, so far from civilisation, who would complain?! It is believed that the upper wing surfaces were also left in US markings. Note also the absence of a fin flash, and the RAAF serial reduced to a single '78' crudely painted under the stabiliser.
(AHM & WA)

✝

IN MEMORIAM

Douglas Boston & Havoc
RAAF

Name	Service No	Rank	Age	Origin	Date	Serial
ATKINS, Henry Lindrum	AUS. 419377	F/O	20	RAAF	20.09.44	A28-53
BONE, Charles Verdun	AUS. 16961	LAC	27	RAAF	14.09.44	A28-61
BORLAND, John Harold	AUS. 405569	F/O	28	RAAF	10.11.42	A28-12
BULLMORE, Herbert James	AUS. 402045	F/L	27	RAAF	29.11.42	A28-20
CLARK, Kenneth Edward	AUS. 435163	F/O	19	RAAF	25.09.44	A28-50
COLLINS, Austin James	AUS. 400871	F/Sgt	30	RAAF	01.06.43	A28-13
COSTIGAN, William Archibald	AUS. 73200	LAC	20	RAAF	14.09.44	A28-61
DAVIDSON, James Ernest	AUS. 406923	F/O	22	RAAF	14.09.44	A28-61
DAWES, Lance	AUS. 414541	Sgt	25	RAAF	06.02.43	A28-21
DAWKINS, Harry Blinman*	AUS. 280791	F/L	27	RAAF	22.07.44	A28-15
EASTWOOD, Basil Gilbert	AUS. 13055	Sgt	31	RAAF	18.03.43	A28-3
EMERTON, James Gibson	AUS. 250283	W/C	26	RAAF	30.01.44	A28-27
GEHRMAN, Ronald Edward	AUS. 43071	F/O	23	RAAF	20.09.44	A28-53
GLEW, Wallis Conrad	AUS. 410973	P/O	21	RAAF	14.09.44	A28-61
GORDON, Francis Colin	AUS. 405047	F/Sgt	22	RAAF	09.02.43	A28-14
GWAYNE, Terence John	AUS. 408648	P/O	23	RAAF	30.01.44	A28-27
HALL, Horace William	AUS. 414486	Sgt	20	RAAF	09.02.43	A28-14
KENWAY, Lesland Arthur	AUS. 405590	F/O	23	RAAF	09.02.43	A28-14
KERR, Roderick Thomas	AUS. 401799	Sgt	29	RAAF	06.02.43	A28-21
KNIGHT, James Bell	AUS. 19067	F/O	25	RAAF	11.10.43	A28-26
LYON, John*	AUS. 401706	F/Sgt	26	RAAF	20.03.43	A28-3
MCKAY, John William	AUS. 405492	Sgt	28	RAAF	29.11.42	A28-20
MCDONALD, Kenneth Roy	AUS. 250430	S/L	n/k	RAAF	26.11.42	A28-22
MOORE, John Eames	AUS. 20932	LAC	23	RAAF	01.06.43	A28-13
MORGAN, Vernon William	AUS. 250550	F/L	25	RAAF	10.11.42	A28-12
MULLENS, Philip Courtney	AUS. 402249	F/L	28	RAAF	01.06.43	A28-13
MURRIE, Glen Inglis	AUS. 416600	F/L	22	RAAF	23.09.44	A28-55
NAPIER, Charles Roland	AUS. 420247	Sgt	24	RAAF	26.11.42	A28-22
NEWTON, William Ellis*	AUS. 250748	F/L	23	RAAF	29.03.43	A28-3
O'NEILL, Thomas Edward	AUS. 407451	F/O	29	RAAF	26.11.42	A28-22
POWER, Ronald Thomas	AUS. 420053	Sgt	22	RAAF	10.11.42	A28-12
RILEY, Erci George Turton	AUS. 411522	P/O	25	RAAF	12.09.43	A28-16
ROWLANDS, George Ivan	AUS. 425223	F/O	25	RAAF	23.09.44	A28-55
SAILL, Norman Henry	AUS. 33313	Sgt	31	RAAF	01.06.43	A28-13
SEMPLE, Douglas George	AUS. 26741	F/Sgt	21	RAAF	12.09.43	A28-15
SMITH, George Trevelyan	AUS. 401793	P/O	31	RAAF	06.02.43	A28-21
STODART, Ian Cameron	AUS. 413801	Sgt	20	RAAF	29.11.42	A28-20
STREET, Frank	AUS. 69438	LAC	33	RAAF	14.09.44	A28-61
THOMAS, Gordon Ronald*	AUS. 417011	F/Sgt	23	RAAF	05.03.44	A28-15
WARREN, John Edward	AUS. 402424	F/O	22	RAAF	25.09.44	A28-50
WILSON, Lindsay Kenneth	AUS. 413921	F/Sgt	26	RAAF	12.09.43	A28-16

Died in captivity

Total: 41

n/k: not known

Douglas Boston Mk. III A28-13 (ex-AL367)
No. 22 Squadron RAAF
Port Moresby (New Guinea), end 1942

Douglas Boston Mk. III A28-9 (ex-AL891)
No. 22 Squadron RAAF
Squadron Leader Charles C. LEARMONTH
Port Moresby (New Guinea), spring 1943

Douglas A-20G-45-DO A28-78
No. 22 Squadron RAAF
Noemfoor Island (NEI), October 1944

SQUADRONS! - The series